WILD ONES
ZEBRAS
by JILL ANDERSON

NorthWord
Minnetonka, Minnesota

As the sun comes up over the plains of Africa, a family of zebras stands and stretches.

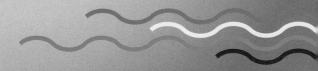

Look at their beautiful striped coats!

No two zebras look exactly alike.

Except for its stripes,
a zebra looks a lot
like a horse.

It has a mane of
stiff hair on its neck
and a tuft of long
hair at the end
of its tail.
It has hard,
black feet
called hooves.

Zebra families live together in groups called herds.

The leader of the herd is always a male, or stallion. He is the father of all the babies in the herd.

The females in
the herd are called
mares. Mares have
one baby, or foal,
at a time. Male
foals are called colts,
and female foals are
called fillies.

A foal never strays far from its mother.

That's because it needs lots of its mother's milk to grow **big** and **strong.**

As foals grow, they start to eat grass and play with other foals.

They jump and push each other, run races, and even play tag!

Zebras spend most of their day eating.

Adult zebras eat **lots** and **lots** of grass. Like people, zebras need plenty of water to drink, too.

Zebras spend part of each day cleaning themselves and each other. They lick and bite their coats to remove dirt and bugs. They talk quietly to other zebras by blowing air through their lips or whinnying.

Lions, hyenas, and other animals like to catch zebras.

So zebras are always watching and listening for danger. If they spot an enemy, they give a loud bark and run away *FAST.*

As daylight fades, the mares and foals lay down to rest.

The stallion sleeps standing up. He will watch over his family until morning comes again.

For Felix, who needed to know more about zebras
(and will soon know more than I do)
—J. A.

Composed in the United States of America
Designed by Lois A. Rainwater • Edited by Kristen McCurry

Text © 2005 by Jill Anderson

NorthWord
Books for Young Readers
11571 K-Tel Drive
Minnetonka, MN 55343
www.tnkidsbooks.com

Photographs © 2005 provided by:
Digital Vision/Punchstock.com: cover, back cover, pp. 1, 20-21; Jim Brandenberg/2003 Minden Pictures: endsheets;
Mitsuaki Iwago/2003 Minden Pictures: pp. 2-3, 24; Frans Lanting/2003 Minden Pictures: pp. 4-5;
Garykramer.net: pp. 6, 8-9, 12-13, 16-17, 21 (hyena); Robin Brandt: pp. 7, 10, 11, 14-15, 18;
Craig Brandt: p. 19; Anup & Manoj Shah: p. 22-23.

Library of Congress Cataloging-in-Publication Data

Anderson, Jill.
Zebras / by Jill Anderson.
p. cm. -- (Wild ones)
ISBN 1-55971-926-5 (hardcover) -- ISBN 1-55971-927-3 (pbk.)
1. Zebras--Juvenile literature. I. Title. II. Series.

QL737.U62A75 2005

599.665'7--dc22   2004030599

Printed in Malaysia
CPSIA Tracking Information: Selangor Darul Ehsan Malaysia. Date of Production: July 2011. Cohort: Batch # 1